Railways

The wheel was discovered so long ago, we have forgotten when it was. Lots of uses have been found for it over the years. Pots can be shaped on a wheel. Driven by wind or water, it can grind corn or saw wood. It can make a clock work. Yet it is only a mere 150 years ago that wheels could first carry us any faster than a horse did. Until then, the wheel as a means of rapid tranport had been something of a disappointment. It stuck in the mud. It bounced people silly on springs, but jarred their spines without them. Then, 150 years ago, a steam engine drove an iron wheel along an iron rail. Scores of people were suddenly hurtled along at 50 kilometres an hour (30 miles per hour) — and survived!

The world was never to be the same again. The first modern transport system, the railway, had been born. It is still with us, and it still has some surprises in store for us, as you will see.

US 'cowcatcher' of the 1860s

The First Trains

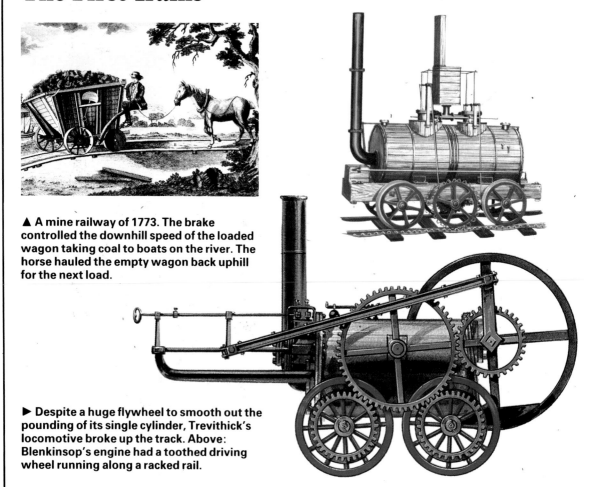

▲ A mine railway of 1773. The brake controlled the downhill speed of the loaded wagon taking coal to boats on the river. The horse hauled the empty wagon back uphill for the next load.

▶ Despite a huge flywheel to smooth out the pounding of its single cylinder, Trevithick's locomotive broke up the track. Above: Blenkinsop's engine had a toothed driving wheel running along a racked rail.

Ever since wheels were invented — no one knows how many thousands of years ago — the search has been on for suitable surfaces for them to run along. Cartwheels make tracks in soft ground, smoothing the way for those that follow. But rain turns rutted tracks to mud, and wheels get stuck in it. Perhaps the first permanent tracks were cut into hard rock. Man-made rutways more than 3000 years old have been found, some linking one line to another through 'points' not unlike modern ones.

When most long-distance transport was by water, miners particularly had to move heavy loads of coal or metal ores to the nearest waterway. Along mine tunnels and from minehead to canal, river or seaport, first wood or stone, later cast-iron tracks were laid for horse-drawn wagons.

Mines and ironworks in Britain were the first to use steam power, to pump flooded workings dry and to work rock-crushing hammers to extract the valuable ores. It was not long before the cleverest managers and engineers, men like Richard Trevithick, John Blenkinsop, William Hedley and George Stephenson, were experimenting with steam locomotives to haul their railway wagons. Their eventual success soon spread steam railways to all parts of the world.

KINGFISHER KINGPINS

The Superbook of
RAILWAYS

David Roberts

KINGFISHER BOOKS

Contents

This revised edition published in 1985 by Kingfisher Books Limited
Elsley House, 24-30 Great Titchfield Street, London W1P 7AD
A Grisewood & Dempsey Company
Originally published in hardcover by Ward Lock Limited in 1980
in the *Wonder Book* series.
Reprinted 1987
© Grisewood & Dempsey Limited 1980, 1985

BRITISH LIBRARY CATALOGUING IN PUBLICATION DATA
Roberts, David, *1926–*
  Railways. — 2nd ed. — (Kingpins)
  1. Railroads — History — Juvenile literature
  I. Title   II. Roberts, David, *1926–*
  Wonder book of railways.   III. Series
  625.1'009   TF148

  ISBN 0-86272-173-3

Edited by Angela Wilkinson
Designed by Keith Groom
Cover designed by the Pinpoint Design Company
Printed in Hong Kong by the South China Printing Co.

Cover: A freight train in Sierra Madre mountains, Mexico.
**Previous page: The *Flying Scotsman*, the first British
locomotive to reach 100 mph (161 km/h).**

Railways

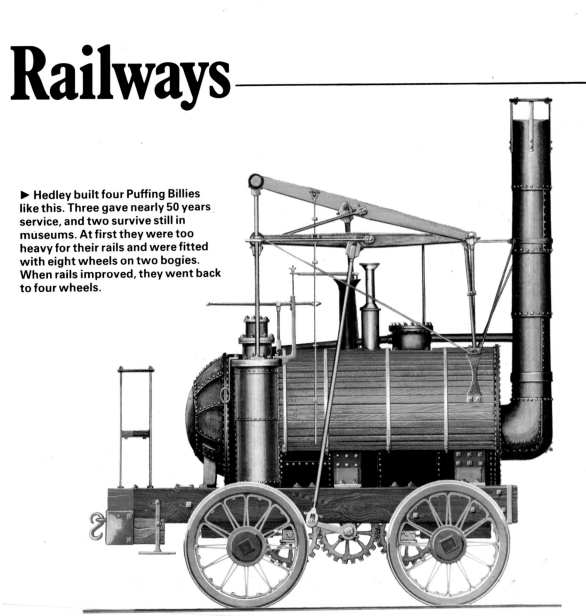

► Hedley built four Puffing Billies like this. Three gave nearly 50 years service, and two survive still in museums. At first they were too heavy for their rails and were fitted with eight wheels on two bogies. When rails improved, they went back to four wheels.

Some Famous Firsts

- **13 Feb 1804**: World's first locomotive, adapted by **Richard Trevithick** from a steam-hammer engine, hauled 10 tonnes of iron and 70 passengers 15 km (9 miles) at 8 km/h (5 mph) on Penydarran Ironworks railway, South Wales, to win a bet for owner Samuel Homfray.
- **1805**: World's first passenger railway service opened in Surrey with horse-drawn carriages.
- **1812**: World's first steam railway began at the Middleton colliery, Yorkshire, using locomotives on a racked rail designed by **John Blenkinsop**. For 30 years, four of them each hauled 100 tonnes of coal at 6 km/h (4 mph) along the 5-km (3-mile) track.
- **1813**: First successful smooth-wheel locomotive, designed by **William Hedley**, ran on smooth rails at Wylam colliery near Newcastle upon Tyne.
- **25 July 1814**: First locomotive designed by **George Stephenson** began work at the Killingworth colliery near Newcastle upon Tyne. Then called *My Lord*, it was later renamed *Blücher* after the Prussian field-marshal at the Battle of Waterloo.
- **9 Aug 1829**: First steam locomotive in America, British-built *Stourbridge Lion*, ran at Honesdale, Pennsylvania, but proved too heavy for the track.
- **1829**: First French steam locomotive was designed and built by **Marc Séguin** for the St Etienne-Lyon line.
- **25 Aug 1830**: First American-built locomotive, *Tom Thumb* by **Peter Cooper**, covered 13 miles (21 km) of the Baltimore & Ohio Railroad in one hour. Slowed on its return by mechanical trouble, it was passed by a horse-drawn train on the adjoining track.

Train of Waggons drawn by a Loco-motive Engine.

The First Railways

The world's first public steam train opened the Stockton and Darlington Railway. It was driven by its chief engineer, George Stephenson. Horsemen with flags led the engine and tender hauling five coal wagons, one of flour, a special owners' coach *Experiment*, six wagons of guests, fourteen of workmen and six more of coal. An average of 13 km/h (8 mph) took them from Shildon colliery to Darlington. Downhill into Stockton, it reached 24 km/h (15 mph), despite an extra 300 hangers-on who had climbed aboard.

▶ *Locomotion,* built at the Stephensons' Newcastle factory and brought by road to Darlington, was first tested the day before the Grand Opening. Then, until 1833, steam was used only for freight, with a horse-drawn coach service for passengers.

▲ The Stockton and Darlington Grand Opening was on 27 September 1825. George Stephenson planned the line with his son, Robert, and John Dixon in 1821. They laid the first rail, of the new wrought iron, at Stockton on May 1822.

The next public railway, from Liverpool to Manchester, ran 48 km (30 miles) through a tunnel and a cutting 28 m (92 ft) deep, over a 9-arch viaduct and 63 other bridges, and across the marsh of Chat Moss. George Stephenson was chosen to build it, though a system of stationary engines hauling trains on ropes was favoured at first. Only when the Stephensons' *Rocket* (below) triumphed at the Rainhill Trials of 8-14 October 1829 was steam locomotion at last accepted. When the line opened on 15 September 1830, no less than eight trains were pulled in procession by locomotives. The day ended in chaos when the MP William Huskisson was run over by *Rocket*. A 50 km/h (31 mph) railway dash failed to save his life. But by then, the Stephensons and the railways were quite unstoppable.

1829.

GRAND COMPETITION

OF

LOCOMOTIVES

ON THE

LIVERPOOL & MANCHESTER RAILWAY.

STIPULATIONS & CONDITIONS

ON WHICH THE DIRECTORS OF THE LIVERPOOL AND MANCHESTER RAILWAY OFFER A PREMIUM OF £500 FOR THE MOST IMPROVED LOCOMOTIVE ENGINE.

▲ The announcement of the contest for steam locomotives won by the Stephensons' *Rocket*.

◄ An early freight train running through Olive Mount Cutting near Liverpool on George Stephenson's line.

▼ The passenger service, which proved more profitable than freight, seen crossing Chat Moss, the marsh many believed would swallow the trains whole.

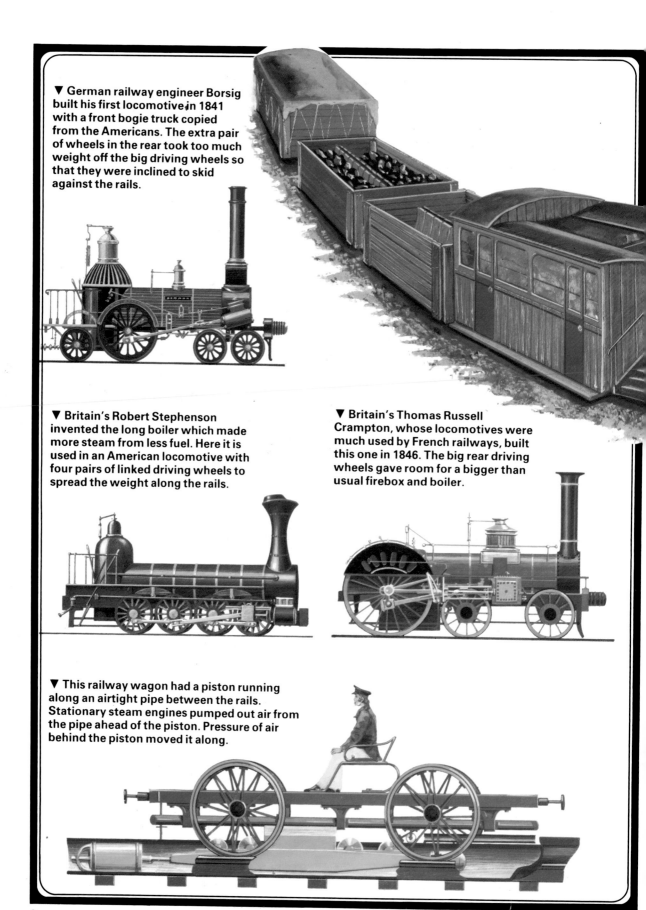

▼ German railway engineer Borsig built his first locomotive in 1841 with a front bogie truck copied from the Americans. The extra pair of wheels in the rear took too much weight off the big driving wheels so that they were inclined to skid against the rails.

▼ Britain's Robert Stephenson invented the long boiler which made more steam from less fuel. Here it is used in an American locomotive with four pairs of linked driving wheels to spread the weight along the rails.

▼ Britain's Thomas Russell Crampton, whose locomotives were much used by French railways, built this one in 1846. The big rear driving wheels gave room for a bigger than usual firebox and boiler.

▼ This railway wagon had a piston running along an airtight pipe between the rails. Stationary steam engines pumped out air from the pipe ahead of the piston. Pressure of air behind the piston moved it along.

This odd-looking train was designed by the French engineer Charles Lartigue and opened in Ireland in 1889. It straddled an A-shaped section of rails. The main weight was taken by the high centre rail, with lower side rails to steady it. Loads had to be kept in rough balance. A farmer taking a cow to market balanced it with two calves, and they balanced each other on the return journey. The line operated for 35 years until lack of profits finally forced it to close down in 1924.

Strange Trains

The spread of railways around the world was much more amazing to the people of the 19th century than the landing of men on the Moon has been to us. We are used to, even bored by, scientific wizardry. Then, the sheer size of the networks was breathtaking. There had been nothing like them since the Great Wall of China.

The need to lay track with no steep hills or sharp bends led to the longest tunnels ever dug, to high embankments and to deep cuttings. Viaducts 30 metres (100 feet) high strode across wide valleys. Iron, and later steel, brought new beauty to the design of bridges. Great iron and glass arcades spanned the main stations and put sparkle into man-made clouds of steam.

Above all, the locomotives with hearts of fire flew across the landscape, throwing off sparks and roaring like dragons. They went at speeds no one had ever thought possible. Indeed, it seemed that the human body could never survive them.

But that was the marvel of the railways. Unlike spaceflight, rail travel was open to all. Soon, the whole civilized world was on the move as never before. Looking back now, we can laugh at some of the locomotives and rail systems of those experimental days. To people then, everything about the railways was new and strange and wonderful.

Some of the wilder ideas may have failed, but fast modern transport had arrived.

Steam Across the World

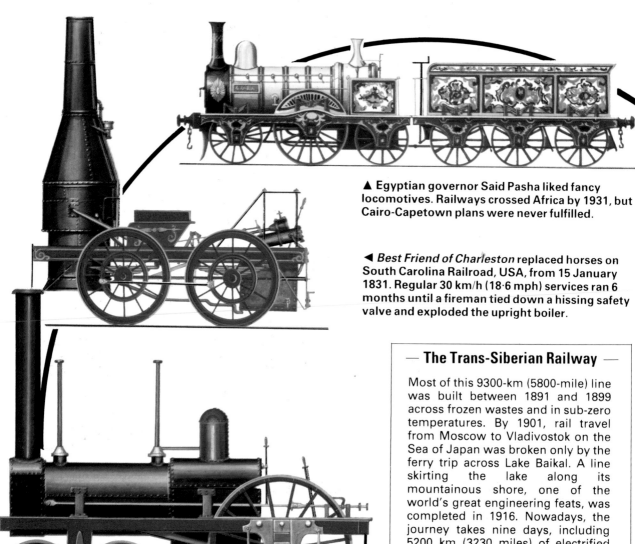

▲ Egyptian governor Said Pasha liked fancy locomotives. Railways crossed Africa by 1931, but Cairo-Capetown plans were never fulfilled.

◀ *Best Friend of Charleston* replaced horses on South Carolina Railroad, USA, from 15 January 1831. Regular 30 km/h (18·6 mph) services ran 6 months until a fireman tied down a hissing safety valve and exploded the upright boiler.

— The Trans-Siberian Railway —

Most of this 9300-km (5800-mile) line was built between 1891 and 1899 across frozen wastes and in sub-zero temperatures. By 1901, rail travel from Moscow to Vladivostok on the Sea of Japan was broken only by the ferry trip across Lake Baikal. A line skirting the lake along its mountainous shore, one of the world's great engineering feats, was completed in 1916. Nowadays, the journey takes nine days, including 5200 km (3230 miles) of electrified line, the longest stretch in the world. In bad weather before the railway opened, it had been known to take travellers two years.

▲ The US *Experiment* of 1832 was the first engine with a bogie, 4-wheel pivoting truck in front.

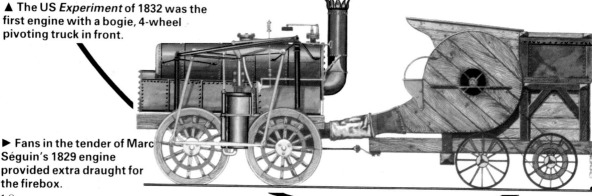

▶ Fans in the tender of Marc Séguin's 1829 engine provided extra draught for the firebox.

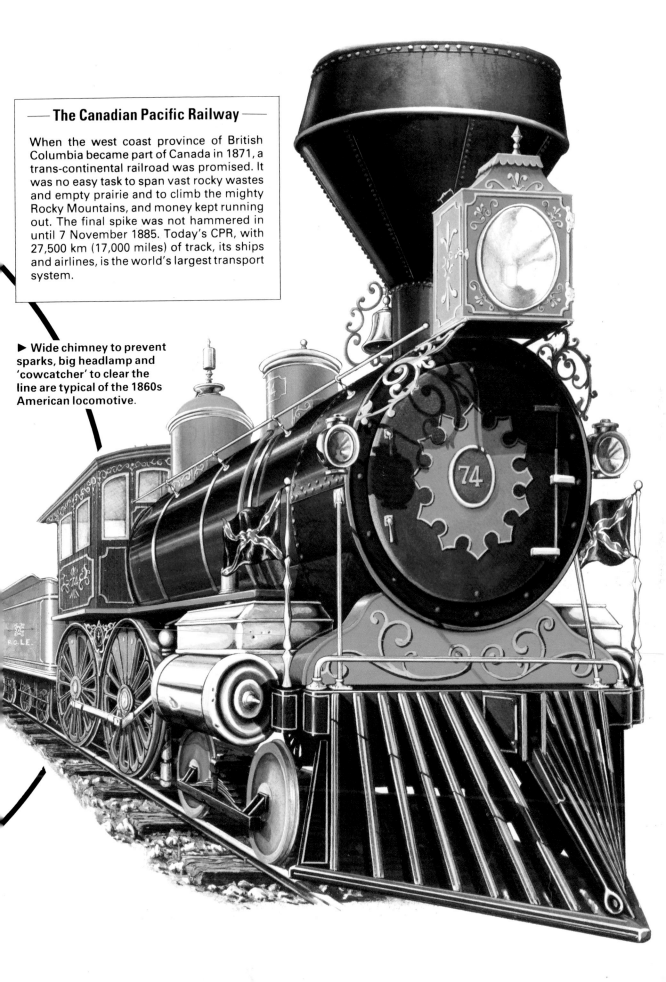

The Canadian Pacific Railway

When the west coast province of British Columbia became part of Canada in 1871, a trans-continental railroad was promised. It was no easy task to span vast rocky wastes and empty prairie and to climb the mighty Rocky Mountains, and money kept running out. The final spike was not hammered in until 7 November 1885. Today's CPR, with 27,500 km (17,000 miles) of track, its ships and airlines, is the world's largest transport system.

▶ Wide chimney to prevent sparks, big headlamp and 'cowcatcher' to clear the line are typical of the 1860s American locomotive.

How a Steam Locomotive Works

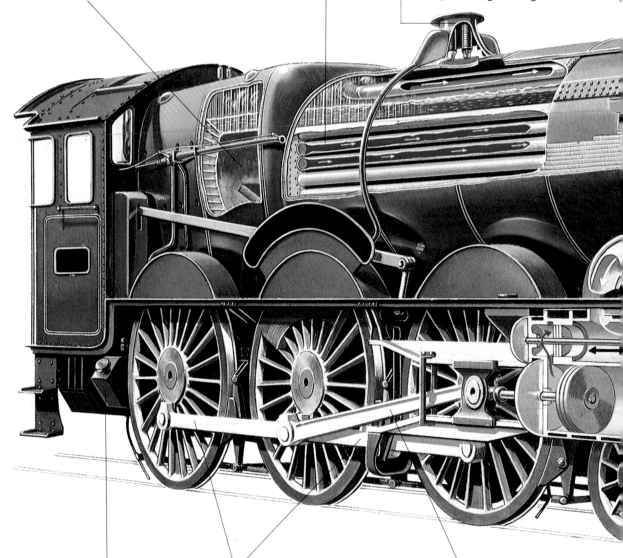

2 The **boiler** in front of the firebox is filled with water to be turned into steam. **Boiler flue tubes** carry hot gases from the firebox through the boiler to heat the water. Steam collects in the space above the water

3 **Safety valve** to let off excess steam

4 The **smokebox** and its chimney draw hot gases through the boiler tubes from the firebox, providing a draught for the fire

1 The **firebox** usually burns coal, sometimes wood or oil

11 A **sand-box** scatters sand on the rails in front of or behind the driving wheels to give them extra grip when starting forward or in reverse

10 **Connecting rods** link front, middle and rear wheels together, making six driving wheels in all

9 The **driving rod** of each piston turns a driving wheel. On this locomotive, two outside cylinders drive the middle pair of driving wheels; two inside cylinders drive the front pair

Trains

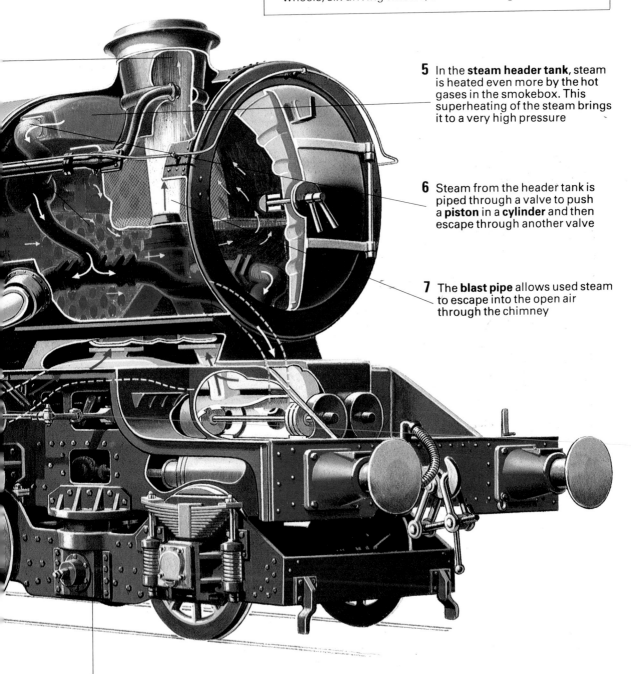

Train Terms

Bogie: A small 4-wheeled truck which pivots so that the coach or engine it carries can go round steep bends.
Wheel code: Locomotives are classified by the arrangement of their wheels. A 4-6-2 locomotive has four leading wheels, six driving wheels, and two trailing wheels.

5 In the **steam header tank**, steam is heated even more by the hot gases in the smokebox. This superheating of the steam brings it to a very high pressure

6 Steam from the header tank is piped through a valve to push a **piston** in a **cylinder** and then escape through another valve

7 The **blast pipe** allows used steam to escape into the open air through the chimney

8 A **bogie truck** with four smaller wheels at the front of the locomotive allows it to take bends smoothly

The Fastest Trains

Records for Steam

- **1893**: First recorded run of 100 mph (161 km/h) made by *Empire State Express* (above) of New York Central and Hudson River Railroad.
- **March 1935**: World record of 174 km/h (108 mph) reached by Pacific *Papyrus* of the LNER.
- **May 1936**: A German 4-6-4 clocked 200·48 km/h (124·5 mph) pulling about 200 tonnes on almost level track.
- **July 1938**: Britain's Pacific A4 class *Mallard* (below) of LNER pulled 7 carriages weighing about 245 tonnes down 1-in-200 gradient at 202·73 km/h (126 mph).

The last item in this list of record breakers is the official all-time speed record for steam trains. Some experts argue that, allowing for the weights and gradients, the German performance of May 1936 was marginally better. There are other contenders, but around 200 km/h seems to be the limit for steam.

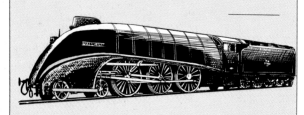

By the end of the 19th century, improvements in couplings between rolling stock and new braking systems brought ever longer and heavier trains. These in turn demanded bigger and better locomotives. For more power, a bigger boiler and a bigger firebox were needed. To support the extra weight, a pair of trailing wheels was added behind the driving wheels. The classic 20th century passenger express had a 4-6-2 arrangement: that is, a 4-wheel bogie in front, 6 coupled driving wheels and a pair of trailing wheels.

For passenger services, it was speed that attracted the customers. Crack expresses vied with each other to reach first the 100 mph (161 km/h) mark and, later, the 200 km/h (124 mph). For freight, weight was more important than speed. To haul the long, heavily-loaded goods trains, it was power that mattered. For this, the biggest of all locomotives were developed.

In the end, size and the amounts of fuel that had to be carried brought an end to steam engines. Even automatic coal-firing to feed those monster appetites failed to save them. To compete with road and air transport, rail turned to electric or diesel motors, even gas-turbines, for its power.

◀ The famous American 4-4-0 locomotives were widely copied in Europe. This British version was among the fastest. It may have been one of the first to haul passenger trains at 100 mph (161 km/h).

▲ This German State Railways engine hauled trains at over 200 km/h (124 mph) to win the steam record in May 1936.

◀ In 1934, London and North Eastern Railway's *Flying Scotsman* made the first 100 mph (161 km/h) run in Britain during one of its regular daily passenger hauls between London and Edinburgh.

▶ Among the constant efforts to run ever faster passenger services, the latest art of streamlining was introduced into the design of many 20th century locomotives. This is the American *Hiawatha* 4–4–2, biggest, fastest, and the last, of the Atlantic breed. The Chicago, Milwaukee, St Paul and Pacific Railroad regularly hauled passenger trains at speeds well above 100 mph (161 km/h) using such magnificent locomotives.

The Biggest Trains

▲ Big Boys like this, the biggest locomotives ever, were built in America in the 1940s. Eight driving wheels were fixed, another eight swivelled. With front and rear bogies, these 4-8-8-4 giants worked on quite light rails, using 22 tonnes of coal and 44 tonnes of water every hour.

▶ Giant locomotives had their heyday in the years between the two World Wars. This one was German and had a horsepower rating of 1950 with a top speed of 140 km/h (87 mph).

Locomotive Sizes Compared

Stephensons' *Rocket* (p 11): 6·60m (21·67ft)

6-8-6 Steam Turbine: 37·49m (123ft)

City of Truro (pp 18-19): 17·19m (56·34ft)

Atlantic *Hiawatha* (p 19): 27·02m (88·67ft)

Chapelon, Europe's most powerful steam loco: 20·38m (66·17ft)

Diesel-electric (pp 30-31): 22·02m (72·26ft)

Big Boy (p 20): 40·48m (132·77ft)

Advanced Passenger Train Power Car (p 38): 21·03m (69ft)

◄ A Beyer-Garratt was a powerful giant on light track with sharp bends in Africa and Australia. It had one swivel truck of driving wheels under a water tank in front, another under a rear fuel tank, with the boiler slung between them. The weight was thus evenly spread along its length.

▼ Mallet locomotives get their name from Frenchman Anatole Mallet who devised a way to drive a rear set of wheels with high pressure steam, and then use the steam again at a lower pressure to drive a set of wheels in front. This Mallet 2-8-8-8-4 of 1914 has three sets of driving wheels.

The Track

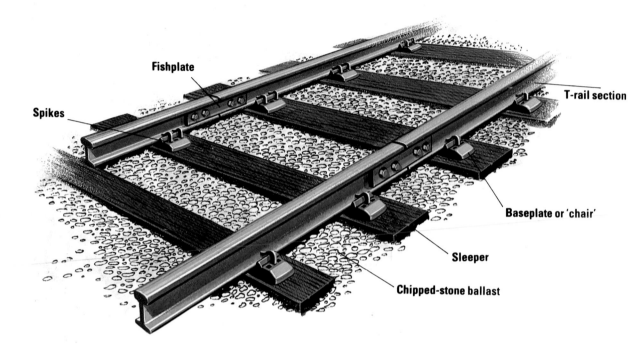

Fishplate

Spikes

T-rail section

Baseplate or 'chair'

Sleeper

Chipped-stone ballast

▲ Most of the world's railways were laid down like this. The ground was made level and firm. Wooden sleepers were laid at short intervals. Lengths of rail were fixed by means of 'chairs' or baseplates spiked into the sleepers. Each length of rail was bolted to the next with a fishplate. Finally, a ballast of stone chips filled in between the sleepers for drainage.

▼ One answer to a steep gradient: three locomotives combine their power to haul a passenger train up a long incline on a New South Wales, Australia, railway.

Track Facts

- **World's widest gauge:** 1·676 m (5·5 ft) in the Indian sub-continent, Chile and Argentina.
- **World's narrowest gauge:** 0·381 m (1·25 ft) used in England on Romney, Hythe and Dymchurch, Railway and on Ravenglass and Eskdale Railway, Cumbria.
- **World's longest line:** 9334 km (5800 miles) across Siberia, from Moscow to Nakhodka, USSR, with 97 stops.
- **World's longest straight line:** 478 km (297 miles) across Nullarbor Plain, Western and South Australia.
- **World's highest standard gauge:** 4817m (15,800 ft) above sea-level on the Morococha Branch at La Cima of Peruvian State Railways, South America.

Railways

The first engineer to plan railway lines for self-propelled vehicles was George Stephenson. In doing so, he laid down two principles that have been followed ever since by most of the world's railway engineers. The first was what became the standard width or gauge between the two lines. Stephenson hit on 4 feet 8½ inches (1·435 m) perhaps because it was the gauge on the colliery tramway where he had begun work on railways. The second principle was that the track should follow as much as possible a level course with only gradual bends.

A metal wheel on a metal track provides the least amount of friction on any form of wheeled transport. This means that the heaviest loads can be carried at the highest speeds on railways. But there must be enough weight to provide the necessary grip for starting, stopping, climbing and descending. The steepest gradient on any smooth-wheeled, smooth-rail track in the world is 1-in-11 between Samala Bridge and Zuni on the Guatemalan State Electric Railway. Of course, there are tight curves of which George Stephenson might not have approved, but these need special articulated locomotives with even the driving wheels mounted on bogies.

▲ A double zig-zag, one of 19 on the Central Railway in Peru. Shunting to and fro, a train can overcome a steep incline.

▲ Toothed wheels must run in a racked rail to climb the Pilatus line in Switzerland.

Engineering

Facts and Feats

The Stephensons and their pupils, such as Joseph Locke and Thomas Brassey, avoided rivers and skirted mountains wherever possible. Railway surveyors always had an eye for economy, for the easy way. They were not always successful. Early railway engineers often ran into underground hazards such as quicksands. The costs could double. But, at least in Britain, a level route was easier to find. In Switzerland, there was often no way round the mountains. Here the Rhaetian Railway bursts from a sheer cliff-face to soar across the valley floor over the Landwasser Viaduct.

As railways advanced across the world, they invented their technology along the way. Cast-iron rails proved too brittle for the pounding wheels. In 1820, just in time for the railway boom, John Birkinshaw of Bedlington Ironworks in Northumberland produced a tougher, rolled out wrought-iron rail. In mid-century America, William Kelly made steel by burning off the carbon in molten iron with blasts of air. The method, perfected in Britain by Henry Bessemer, made cheap steel rails available from 1860.

Bridge-building advanced as rapidly. Caissons, kept watertight by compressed air, allowed workmen to build piers on river-beds. In 1841, John Roebling, a German immigrant to America, patented a method of stretching steel wires over towers and binding them together. A deck hung from these cables gave the whole structure the name of suspension bridge. Similarly, the cantilever method of building outwards from central piers was devised by J. B. Eads for the three 150-metre steel arches of the bridge over the Mississippi at St. Louis, Missouri.

Tunnelling techniques also improved. A tunnel under Mont Cenis to link Lyon in France by rail to Turin in Italy was begun in 1857. Blasting with gunpowder went on for 13 years. The St Gotthard tunnel, begun in 1872, took half the time using Alfred Nobel's new dynamite.

Tunnels and Bridges

- **World's longest railway tunnel**: 27·8 km (17·3 miles) on London's underground network from Morden to East Finchley via Bank, opened in 1939.
- **World's longest mainline tunnel**: 19·82 km (12·3 miles) Simplon II between Italy and Switzerland, opened in 1922.
- **World's longest rail tunnel underwater**: 18·6 km (11·6 miles) Shin Kanmon tunnel, Honshū to Kyūshū, Japan, opened 1974.

Due to be completed some time during 1985 is the 53.9 km (33.5 miles) Seikan Rail Tunnel between Honshū Island and Hokkaidō Island, Japan.
- **World's longest rail bridge**: 7 km (4·4 miles) Huey P Long Bridge, Metairie, Louisiana, USA, opened in 1935.
- **World's highest rail bridge**: 132·5 m (435 ft) above River Sioule, Fades, Clermont-Ferrand, France, opened in 1909.

The Firth of Forth bridge, opened 1890, used 55,000 tonnes of steel cast in foundries set up on shore. The two cantilever arches either side of Inchgarvie island left gaps of 107 m (351 ft). These were bridged by building out towards a central meeting point. So accurately was it planned that small fires of wood shavings were enough to expand the metal and slip the last rivets in place.

21

Famous Routes

In America, a coast-to-coast railroad was an early dream. After the Civil War, the Central Pacific began to push east from Sacramento, California. With local labour diverted by the gold rush, they imported men from China. It was Chinese coolies, fearless and hard-working, who blasted a path through the Sierra Nevada mountains. Meanwhile, the Union Pacific thrust westward from the Omaha, Nebraska, railhead across the Wyoming prairie, fighting the Plains Indians all the way.

With government funding based on mileage, the name of the game was speed.

Expected to take 14 years, the two lines met after six years. In the wilds of Utah, a ceremonial last spike was hammered in, and CP locomotive *Jupiter* touched fenders with UP No 119.

American railroads opened up unknown country. Railways in the Old World had to compete with existing transport. Comfort was as important as speed. Some lines built up the prestige of luxury hotels. Carrying diplomats to China, the Trans-Siberian Express provided sleeping cars, bathrooms, a lounge with a piano, a gymnasium and a church car on Sunday. French wagons-lit

◀ The Canadian Pacific Railroad's express *Canadian* on a 70·5-hour 4636-km (2860-mile) run from Montreal across the Rocky Mountains, where an extra locomotive is added, to Vancouver.

▶ The German *Rheingold,* a Trans-Europ express on part of the network linking more than 100 of the principal cities of Europe with a computerized booking service.

▲ The eastward and westward halves of the world's first transcontinental railroad met at Promontory, Utah, USA, on 10 May 1869.

Centre right: A USSR Trans-Siberian express on its 9300-km (5800-mile) 9-day journey from Moscow across the steppes of Asia to the Sea of Japan.

became famous for food. The Paris-Istanbul Orient Express won a romantic reputation like an ocean liner.

Greater comfort is the one remaining competitive edge that trains have over airlines. Canadian Pacific expresses are mobile three-star hotels, complete with a cinema. The US nationalized railroad, Amtrak, on its *Empire Builder* between Chicago and Seattle, has colour TV and two cinemas, with 25 stewards to look after up to 323 passengers.

These are crests of some early private railway companies. Most countries have now nationalized their railways since they need subsidies to face competition from both road and air transport systems.

Running the Railways

Ever since more than one locomotive has run on the same line, some form of traffic control has been necessary. At first, railway police marched up and down the track, waving flags at engine drivers to halt them or move them on. Later, the mechanical semaphore signalling system was introduced. Arms mounted on posts could be moved up and down by levers, at first from the foot of the post, later from a more remote signal box. The first points to direct a train from one line to another were worked by the drivers. Then these, too, were connected by levers and cables to the nearest signal box.

▼ A modern signal box switchboard controls a large section of track. A signalman flicks electric switches to set points and change signals as lights show him where each train is.

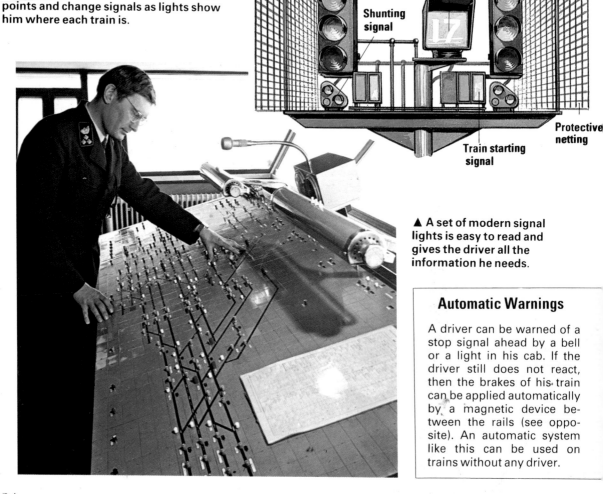

Signal lights in four colours

Route number

Shunting signal

Train starting signal

Protective netting

▲ A set of modern signal lights is easy to read and gives the driver all the information he needs.

Automatic Warnings

A driver can be warned of a stop signal ahead by a bell or a light in his cab. If the driver still does not react, then the brakes of his train can be applied automatically by a magnetic device between the rails (see opposite). An automatic system like this can be used on trains without any driver.

A signalman in charge of a signal box used to control all the trains to enter his section of the rail network. The new invention of the electric telegraph was used to signal from one signal box to the next.

The old signal box with its rows of huge, shining levers that moved semaphore signals and points mechanically is passing. The modern signalman works a switchboard. He signals drivers with lights alongside the track, and with bells and lights inside the driver's cab. He can even use remote control on the locomotive itself.

Accidents still happen, of course, but rarely because of a breakdown in the system. Usually, human failure is the cause of a modern rail disaster. The list gives all the major rail disasters world-wide over a ten-year period. It shows that fatal accidents are rare. Taking into account the vast numbers of people and the large amount of freight moved, modern railways seem safer than most other forms of transport now available.

Disasters

- **20 April 1966:** Locomotive explosion, Lumding Junction, India, 55 dead.
- **6 June 1967:** Collision with petrol truck, Langenweddingin, E. Germany, 82 dead.
- **15 July 1969:** Collision near Jaipur, India, 85 dead.
- **16 Feb 1970:** Crash, North Nigeria, 150 dead.
- **17 June 1972:** Tunnel crash, Soissons, France, 107 dead.
- **28 Feb 1975:** Underground crash in London, England, 41 dead.
- **8 August 1980:** Passenger and freight train collision near Torun, Poland, 62 dead.
- **6 June 1981:** Crowded train fell off bridge into river in Bihar State, India, 268 dead.

▼ The magnetic device between the rails that automatically applies the brakes when needed.

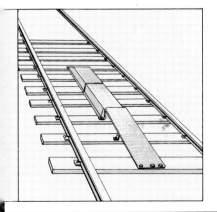

Safety on the Rails

▼ This was the scene near London, England, when an excursion train jumped the rails going round a sharp bend in the track. Four people were killed and 29 injured. The cause of the accident was driving too fast into the bend.

Diesel Trains

When he built the Liverpool and Manchester railway, George Stephenson argued in favour of steam locomotives. Some directors wanted stationary engines spaced along the line to pull trains on cables along each section. A similar choice is available today. Trains can either make their own power in diesel or diesel-electric loco- motives; or they can pick up power from a third rail or overhead wires. In 1830, *Rocket* and steam locomotion triumphed. Today there is no outright winner.

Rudolph Diesel, a German born in Paris, made his first successful engine in 1897. It was different from other internal combus- tion engines in using oil instead of petrol and in having no spark plugs. In petrol engines, a mixture of air and petrol vapour drawn into the cylinder is exploded by an electric spark. In a diesel, air is pumped in alone and compressed by the piston to raise its temperature. At the top of the compression stroke, oil is injected. By then, the air is hot enough to explode the oil, forcing the cylinder down again.

The railbus, locomotive and passenger coach in one, and the railcar towing one or

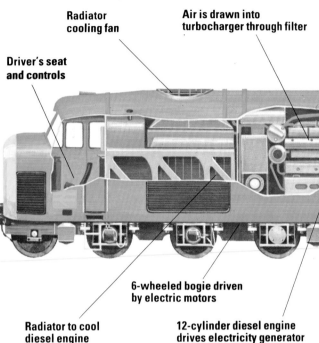

Radiator cooling fan

Air is drawn into turbocharger through filter

Driver's seat and controls

6-wheeled bogie driven by electric motors

Radiator to cool diesel engine

12-cylinder diesel engine drives electricity generator

more coaches, both popular on European branch lines, use low-powered diesels to drive the wheels directly. So do shunting locomotives. Passenger trains and the big goods trains of North America are often hauled by several high-powered diesels. But most common is the locomotive with a diesel engine driving an electric generator. This, in turn, powers electric motors which drive each set of bogie wheels separately. Electric motors can bring a locomotive to top speed much quicker than a diesel by itself, a great advantage to a passenger train stopping at stations all along the way.

◀ A German diesel-electric locomotive. The chimney is for exhaust fumes from the engine.

▶ A Western Pacific freight train is hauled through Feather River Canyon by four diesel locomotives. Sometimes extra power units, called slaves, are put among the wagons and radio-controlled from the leading locomotive.

Railways

Turbocharger, worked by the engine's exhaust gases, forces air into cylinders

Assistant driver's seat

Double-glazed windscreen

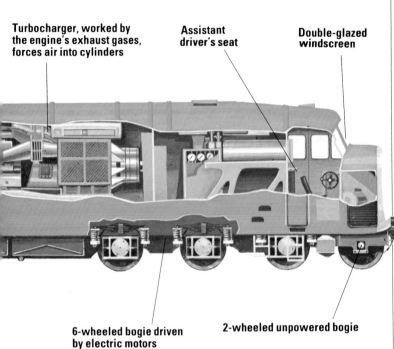

6-wheeled bogie driven by electric motors

2-wheeled unpowered bogie

A diesel shunting locomotive.

Diesel Firsts

- **1912**: World's first diesel locomotive built in Germany.
- **1913**: World's first diesel-electric railcar in service in Sweden. It ran until 1939.
- **1925**: World's first mainline diesel locomotive, designed by Russian Lomonossov, built in Germany.
- **1928**: North America's first mainline diesel in service on Canadian National Railways.
- **1932**: World's first 100 mph (161 km/h) diesel train *Flying Hamburger* in regular service. It once reached 200 km/h (124 mph).

Electric Trains

Electric trains pick up along the way the power to drive them, and so have no fuel to carry. This makes them lighter and faster than other rail transport. For most of this century, electric trains have held the world rail speed record. The world's fastest rail services run on electrified lines. Diesel-electric locomotives may have become the work-horses of the railways, but electric power units are the greyhounds.

Electricity has none of the noxious fumes of diesel, nor the soot of steam. It can be used in tunnels and city centres without air pollution or undue noise. But the track is expensive to put down and maintain. In this rapidly changing world, routes may have to be moved more readily. The speed and economy of diesel and diesel-electric are improving all the time. Meanwhile, pure electric trains experiment with the linear induction motor, using magnetic forces for propulsion. As the fastest and safest form of transport on land, rail may be poised for a breakthrough in the future.

Electric Firsts and Feats

- **31 May 1879**: World's first electric tramway, designed by Werner von Siemens, opened at Berlin Trades Exhibition carrying 30 passengers at 6·5 km/h (4 mph).
- **1883**: World's first electric railway between Portrush and Giant's Causeway, N. Ireland, opened. It was designed by Sir William Siemens, Werner's brother who had settled in England.
- **1895**: World's first mainline electric railway began operation along 5·6 km (3·5 miles) of Baltimore and Ohio Railroad, through Baltimore, Maryland, USA. Huge electric locomotives hauled steam trains, including their locomotives, through tunnels under the city.
- **1901**: A Siemens and Halske electric train set world rail speed record of 162·6 km/h (100·7 mph).
- **1903**: Siemens and Halske electric locomotives lifted the world rail speed record to 210 km/h (130 mph).
- **1955**: Two French National Railways electric locomotives hauled 3-coach trains at 330·8 km/h (205·5 mph) for a distance of 2·8 km (1·74 miles), a record on ordinary track that has never been beaten.
- **28 March 1974**: World rail speed record was set up by an electric Linear Induction Motor Research Vehicle on a 10-km (6·2-mile) test track at Pueblo, Colorado, USA, reaching 376·9 km/h (234·2 mph).

► A Swiss mountain railway train collecting power from overhead electric cables. Because of the gradient, this locomotive uses a toothed driving wheel which engages with a racked rail in the centre of the track. Electric motors are ideal for this kind of light railway with steep slopes, particularly in a country with lots of cheap hydro-electric power.

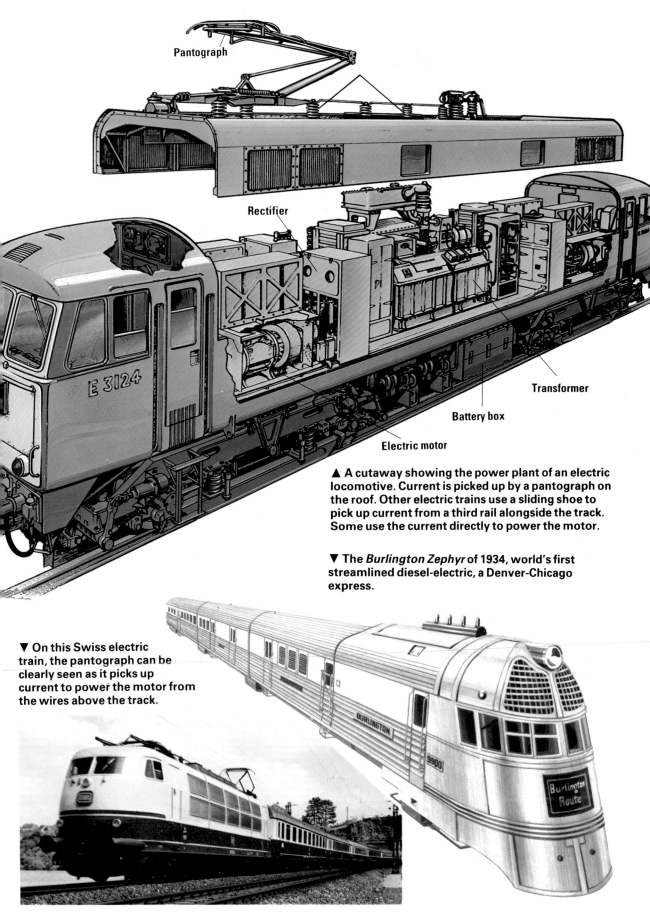

Pantograph

Rectifier

E 3124

Transformer

Battery box

Electric motor

▲ A cutaway showing the power plant of an electric locomotive. Current is picked up by a pantograph on the roof. Other electric trains use a sliding shoe to pick up current from a third rail alongside the track. Some use the current directly to power the motor.

▼ The *Burlington Zephyr* of 1934, world's first streamlined diesel-electric, a Denver-Chicago express.

▼ On this Swiss electric train, the pantograph can be clearly seen as it picks up current to power the motor from the wires above the track.

BURLINGTON

9900

Burlington Route

▲ A controller, in radio contact with marshalling yard staff, trips points to bring together wagons with the same destination. Big yards, like the one on the right, may be controlled by computer.

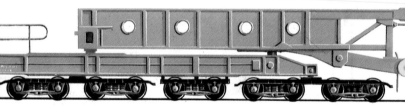

Freight Trains

Road and air transport now carry much of the cargo previously taken by rail. Yet rail is still the best means of hauling bulk such as coal, metal ores and many foodstuffs over medium to long distances. It was the first to use special vehicles designed for particular jobs: refrigerated box-cars for food, tankers for bulk liquids like milk and chemicals, hopper-cars that tip sideways for unloading coal, and many more.

More recently, railways became essential links in the world-wide chains of container transportation. Lorry-sized boxes stacked with a variety of goods are taken by road to the nearest container terminal where they are loaded on the railway flat-cars. They go by rail to the docks for shipping abroad. Locked against theft, containers need not be opened until they reach their destination.

Railways lost work to the roads because of their cumbersome methods of directing a particular wagon through the network. Now, with the aid of computers, fewer marshalling yards can handle more rolling stock. The sorting of it into trains and the speeding of goods on their way has much improved. Railways are fighting with the most modern equipment to win back customers and to rid our roads of the thundering juggernauts.

▲ Loading freight into standard-size containers to be lifted by crane onto flat-cars makes it easier for the system to be controlled from a computer.

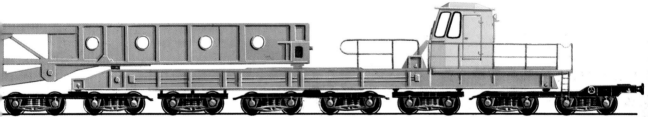

▲ Two 32-wheel trucks of a special transporter spread the payload weight slung between them.

▼ Volkswagen cars transported on a 3-decker freight wagon of Canadian National Railways.

Monorail

The monorail has been around for nearly a hundred years. The Listowel and Ballybunion Railway in County Kerry, Ireland (page 9), was the first and ran for thirty-five years. The Schwehebahn at Wüppertal in West Germany opened in 1901 and has been running ever since. Each of these represents one of the two different kinds still being experimented with throughout the world.

The Irish one straddled a line raised on A-sections. The locomotive had two boilers, one on each side of the line. The passenger coaches had compartments on either side, and wagons were similarly divided. Both goods and passengers had to be evenly balanced. Even so, it was found necessary to have small balancing wheels running on lesser rails lower down on the arms of the A. Strictly speaking, it was a three-rail system.

Since then, the straddled monorail has been much improved. Swedish engineer Dr

Axel L. Wenner, working in Germany, invented the Alweg system shown here. Pairs of vertical wheels run along the top of a rail to take the train's weight. Pairs of horizontal wheels, including driving wheels, run along the sides, keeping the whole train balanced.

At Wüppertal, several towns adjoin each other in a river valley with steep sides. The river is too shallow and rocky for boats. The Schwehebahn was built to run above it, following its winding course for most of the way. Arched supports carry pairs of rails, one for each direction. Coaches hang from bogies running along the top of a rail and powered from a live cable beside it.

Above or alongside other traffic routes, monorails are cheap to erect and run. They can provide extra commuter lines, carrying people swiftly into and out of city centres, relieving pressure on crowded streets. They can even be put underground.

◄ The Wüppertal Schwehebahn, the world's oldest monorail. The section shown here runs above a city street, where it looks unsightly and is noisy so close to homes. In the narrow river valley of the Wüpper, an underground railway is impracticable, but where the Schwehebahn runs above the river it looks very dramatic and quite modern.

► This Japanese monorail runs 13 km (8 miles) from Tokyo city centre to Haneda airport. It uses the Alweg system shown in the diagram. The rail section, in red, carries the weight-supporting wheels on top, and the balancing and driving wheels on the sides. Rubber tyres increase friction but provide a smoother ride.

► This monorail runs through the zoo gardens of Ueno Park, Tokyo, Japan. The picture clearly shows bogie trucks running along a reinforced concrete beam which is the single rail. Coaches hang from arms curving down from one side of each bogie.

▼ A side view of the Ueno Park monorail in Japan, showing its height from the ground. These coaches are of a newer design than those in the picture above.

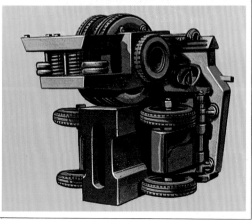

◄ British Rail's new Advanced Passenger Train with electric or gas-turbine power tops 250 km/h (155 mph) and tilts when it goes fast into a bend.

Speeding into the Future

Railways, isolated from other traffic, can travel safely at very high speeds. But ordinary power sources and track have just about reached their limits. The steel wheel on the steel rail was once thought to reduce to a minimum the friction between a vehicle and the surface it ran along. When the hovercraft appeared, almost friction-free on its cushion of air, the hovertrain was not far behind.

Even more exciting are the new ideas for using magnetic forces. Magnetism has the power to repel as well as attract; and magnetic forces are created when an electric current runs through a wire. These are the forces used in ordinary electric motors. A coil magnetized by electricity is made to spin between the poles of other electro-magnets that repel it alternately. Professor Eric Laithwaite of London University has stretched the central coil along the railway line itself. Electro-magnets placed in a locomotive are repelled by it so that the locomotive is driven along the track. Because the coil is stretched along the *line* and because magnetism is *induced* in it by a current of electricity, the Professor's invention is known as the linear induction motor.

Magnetic repulsion can even be made to lift a train like a hovercraft's cushion of air. It needs very powerful magnetism. Certain metals have much less resistance to electricity at very low temperatures. They become superconductors. Current will flow in them almost indefinitely. Using a superconductor in an electromagnet, forces can be created strong enough to lift a whole train. The system is called magnetic levitation (meaning lift) or maglev for short. The UK, USA and Japan have prototypes.

▲ French National Railway's new train uses an aircraft's gas-turbine engine to reach a top speed well over 300 km/h (186 mph).

► This monorail hovertrain is French and topped 375 km/h (233 mph), though its propeller, driven by a gas-turbine engine, is too noisy for commercial use.

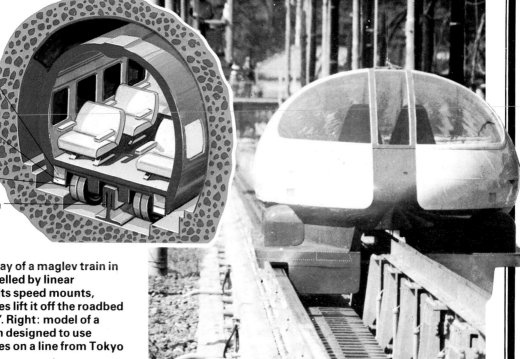

quid helium at a ry low temperature

ectro-magnets oled to become perconductors

heels running on uminium roadbed

agnetized aluminium l for propulsion linear induction

Above: cutaway of a maglev train in a tunnel, propelled by linear induction. As its speed mounts, magnetic forces lift it off the roadbed so that it 'flies'. Right: model of a Japanese train designed to use magnetic forces on a line from Tokyo to Osaka.

Overground,

Mountain Railways

As railway engineers gained experience, their confidence grew. There was almost nowhere they dared not build a railway. The world's steepest smooth rail climbed by smooth wheels is a 1–in–11 rise in Guatemala. Much steeper slopes need help from either rack or cable.

The locomotive on a rack railway has a toothed driving wheel slotted into a racked rail, usually between the other two. The first steam locomotive in regular use, built by Blenkinsop, worked on a rack on level track.

When Sylvester Marsh built his Cog Railway up Mount Washington, New Hampshire, USA, in 1869, he went back to the rack idea. His railway is still running. The oldest European rack railway, an average 1-in-3 up the Righi in Switzerland, was built in 1872. Early racks were like ladders. Then in 1882, Dr Roman Apt invented a double-racked rail, each step on either side facing a gap on the other.

There is no locomotive on a funicular or cable railway. Two coaches on separate tracks are attached to either end of a cable which runs over a pulley at the top. One descends, the other rises. The descending coach can be weighted with water, as on the Lynton-Lynmouth funicular in Devon, England, or the pulley can be driven by an electric motor.

San Francisco cablecars have endless chains moving in slots between the rails. A driver uses levers to hook on to one, to disengage and to hook on to the next. More dramatic than any is the cablecar slung between tall pylons striding up some of the world's most spectacular mountain crags.

Underground

▲ For an eagle's-eye view of the dizzy Alpine heights, the cableway or téléphérique may not strictly be a railway but is certainly an experience!

Above right: San Francisco cablecars are unique to the steep streets of that hilly city. Passengers help to push them round on the turntable at the terminus.

◄ A funicular railway with one of its stepped coaches on its climb up the steep slopes of Niesen Kulm in the Swiss Alps.

► Britain's only rack railway climbs 7·5 km (4·8 miles) from Llanberis to the top of Snowdon, the highest mountain in Wales.

Underground Railways

Railways have had tunnels from the beginning. Hardly a line of any length does not have to plunge through hill or mountain. On railway networks, deep cuttings and bridges abound. The first wholly underground railway was in fact a long bridge built to provide rapid transit between three of London's mainline termini: Paddington, Euston and King's Cross. At least, it was built like a bridge. First, the road that ran by all three stations was dug up to a considerable depth. In the bottom of this great ditch, the railway lines were laid and then built over with brick arches. The carriage road was relaid on top of the arches.

Steam locomotives on this Metropolitan Line, opened in 1863, were designed to eat their own smoke. The condensers fitted to do the job never really worked. Tunnels between stations filled with smoke that drifted into the stations themselves. Conductors were employed to patrol the platforms, calling out the names of the stations. Passengers, peering out from the high windows, could see only a grey fog.

The first electric underground railway, the City and South London, was opened in 1890. Not only did it solve the smoke problem, it was the first railway to be tunnelled wholly underground. The tunnel, circular in section, carried the first of what Londoners came to call tube trains. The advantage of underground railways in cities, freed from traffic jams on the surface, had been triumphantly proved by the Metropolitan Line. Now, new tunnelling techniques could drive railways almost anywhere deep underground, below buildings, sewers, and rivers. Where London led, the major cities of the world have been following ever since.

Probably, city underground systems will become the first fully automated railways. Travellers already buy tickets from machines and have them checked automatically at the barriers. Moving staircases, even moving passageways, carry them to the trains. The trains themselves can be programmed by a computer to start, stop, open and close doors, even to deal with emergencies, without the need for drivers, guards or station staff.

◀ A photograph of the 1863 opening of the Metropolitan Line in London, and an old print of one of its steam trains on wide-gauge track.

▲ A station in San Franscisco's Bay Area Rapid Transit System known as BART for short.

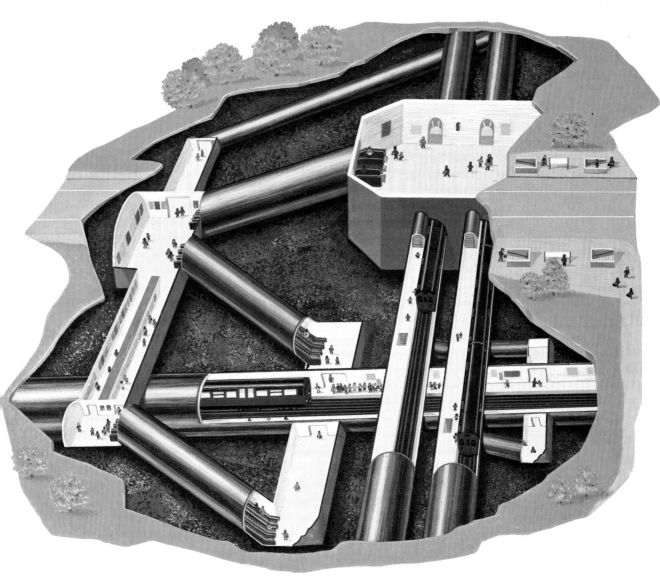

▲ Here is a cutaway view into an underground railway station where two lines cross each other. It shows the entrances from the street, the ticket hall, the escalators, staircases, passages and subways leading to the trains. This entire system could be wholly automated.

Facts and Firsts Underground

- **10 January 1863**: World's first underground railway, the London Metropolitan Line, opened.
- **1890**: World's first electric underground railway, the City and South London, passing beneath the bed of the River Thames, opened.
- **27 October 1904**: America's first underground railway opened in New York City.
- **1927**: World's first driverless underground railway, designed to carry mailbags for the London Post Office, began operations.
- The world's most extensive public underground railway system is in London with a route total of 405 km (252 miles). Its greatest depth is 67·3 m (220 ft); its longest route without a change of trains is 54·8 km (34 miles) between Epping and West Ruislip.
- The world's busiest underground railway is the New York City subway with a route total of 381 km (237 miles) and well over two billion passengers a year. Its 475 stations are set closer together than London's 278.
- London's Victoria Line can carry 50,000 people an hour in trains spaced at 2-minute intervals.

Index

Numbers in **bold type** refer to illustrations.

Acknowledgements

Photographs: 4, 6 Science Museum; 7 Radio Times Hulton Picture Library; 17 Keystone; 18 Victor Hand; 19 Brian Fawcett *top*, Swiss National Tourist Office *bottom*, 20 Swiss Railways; 22 Canadian Pacific Railways; 22/23 Union Pacific Railway; 23 German Federal Railways *top*, Novosti *centre*; 24 Austrian Railways; 24/5 British Rail; 25 Keystone; 26 German Railways; 27 Victor Hand; 28 Swiss Railways; 29 ZEFA; 30 Canadian Pacific; 30/1 SNCF; 31 ZEFA *top*, J. Allan Cash *bottom*, 32, 33 ZEFA; 34 British Rail; 35 SNCF *top*, Japan Information Services *bottom*; 36, 37 ZEFA; 38 BART *right*.
Artwork: Mike Atkinson, Dick Eastland, Richard Hook, Tony Richards, Ron Jobson, Tom Brittain, Michael Trim, John Hofer.

Picture Research: Penny Warn and Jackie Cookson